HR Approved Ways to Deal With Stupid Coworkers

How to Say All The Things You Want To Say At Work But Can't

Corr Prett

SWEET HARMONY PRESS

HR Approved Ways to Deal With Stupid Coworkers: How To Say All the Things You Want to Say At Work But Can't

Copyright © 2025 by Corr Prett and Sweet Harmony Press

All rights reserved. No part of this publication may be reproduced, distributed, or transmitted in any form or by any means, including photocopying, recording, or other electronic or mechanical methods, without the prior written permission of the publisher, except in the case of brief quotations embodied in critical reviews and certain other noncommercial uses permitted by copyright law. For permission requests, write to the publisher at the address below.

Cover art:
ID 131158049 | © Zdenek Sasek | Dreamstime.com
ID 164214288 | © Zdenek Sasek | Dreamstime.com

Sweet Harmony Press
info@sweetharmonypress.com

Ordering Information:
Quantity sales. Special discounts are available on quantity purchases by corporations, associations, and others. For details, contact the publisher at the address above.

Print ISBN: 978-1-948713-55-9
Ebook ISBN: 978-1-948713-56-6
Hardcover ISBN: 978-1-948713-57-3

Disclaimer:
This book is for entertainment and informational purposes only. The author and publisher do not guarantee that the strategies and techniques described in this book will be successful in every situation. The author and publisher shall have neither liability nor responsibility to any person or entity with respect to any loss or damage caused, or alleged to be caused, directly or indirectly by the information contained in this book. Any resemblance to actual coworkers, living or professionally exhausted, is purely coincidental.

Sweet Harmony Press
August 2025

Join our email list to get all the latest news and book announcements.

If you enjoy this book, please consider leaving a review on amazon.com.

Thank you!

Contents

Full Disclaimer	IV
Introduction	VII
1. Welcome to Your "Conflict-Free" Workplace (Just Kidding, It's Chaos with Bad Coffee)	1
2. How to Identify the Problem (Spoiler Alert: It's Definitely Not You)	5
3. HR-Approved Phrases for Handling Coworkers Who Suck	9
4. Workplace Species: A Field Guide to Office Creatures	15
5. How to Write a Complaint So Good, HR Will Frame It	21
6. Passive-Aggressive Communication Styles Ranked from "Mildly Petty" to "Requires Intervention"	27
7. Conflict Role Play: How to Address Issues Directly Without Having a Nervous Breakdown	33
8. Performance Review Prep: How to Spin "I Survived This Year" into "Exceeds Expectations"	39
9. Meetings That Could've Been Emails and Other Crimes Against Productivity	45
10. Team Building Activities and Other Forms of Psychological Warfare	51
11. A Beginner's Guide to Boundary-Setting: Say No Without Saying "F* This Job"	57
12. How to Quit Mentally Without Getting Fired Physically	61

Full Disclaimer

IMPORTANT: Please Read Before Proceeding

This book is intended for **entertainment purposes only** and should not be considered professional, legal, or career advice. While the situations and strategies described may seem familiar (perhaps painfully so), this work is primarily meant to provide humor, perspective, and emotional validation for the universal experience of workplace frustration.

Professional Guidance Recommended: For serious workplace issues including harassment, discrimination, hostile work environments, or other significant professional concerns, please consult with qualified professionals such as:

- Human Resources representatives
- Employment attorneys
- Licensed career counselors
- Workplace mediators
- Mental health professionals

Your Mileage May Vary: Every workplace, company culture, and professional situation is unique. What works as a humorous anecdote in this book may not be appropriate or effective in your specific circumstances. Always use your best judgment and consider the potential consequences of any communication or action in your particular work environment.

Not Actual HR Policy: The "HR-approved" phrases and techniques in this book are satirical observations about corporate communication, not official HR guidance. When in doubt about appropriate workplace behavior or communication, refer to your company's actual policies and procedures.

Mental Health Matters: If workplace stress is significantly impacting your mental health, relationships, or quality of life, please seek support from qualified mental health professionals. This book is not a substitute for proper counseling or therapy.

Legal Disclaimer: The author and publisher are not responsible for any consequences that may result from applying the strategies, phrases, or approaches described in this book. All workplace decisions and communications are made at your own discretion and risk.

Remember: Sometimes the best workplace advice is knowing when to seek help from qualified professionals rather than trying to handle everything with humor and sarcasm (though both certainly have their place).

Now, with that said... let's learn how to survive the beautiful chaos of modern office life with your sanity mostly intact.

Introduction

How Do You Deal With a Coworker Who Treats Deadlines Like Suggestions and Teamwork Like a Blood Sport?

Short answer: You evolve. Like a superhero origin story, but instead of getting bitten by a radioactive spider, you develop an immunity to workplace nonsense and the ability to smile while plotting.

Long answer: You learn the ancient art of professional survival in an environment where "synergy" is a real word people say with straight faces, and someone named Brad from Marketing thinks he's a "disruptor" because he uses Comic Sans in presentations.

Whether you're trapped in a 47-minute meeting about a meeting you're going to have about scheduling another meeting, fielding passive-aggressive emails from Todd in Finance (who signs everything "Best," but clearly means "Worst"), or trying not to lose your actual mind during a trust fall with Karen from HR—this laugh-until-you-cry guide will help you keep your cool, your job, and your ability to make eye contact at the coffee machine.

Inside this HR-safe-but-barely survival manual, you'll learn:

- How to write an email that says "Stop it" without actually saying "Stop it" (or anything that rhymes with "Stop it")

- What to do when someone "accidentally" takes credit for your work (again, Janet, AGAIN)

- Passive-aggressive phrases that sound professional but sting like a paper cut from a performance review

- Real-life coworker archetypes, from The Oversharer Who Thinks Your Cubicle Is a Therapist's Office to The Credit Vulture Who Circles Your Accomplishments Like a Hungry Buzzard

- How to survive your performance review without throwing anything (including yourself out the window)

- The art of professional boundary-setting that doesn't require a law degree or witness protection

- Meeting survival tactics that will save your sanity and your calendar

- **And most importantly: how to mentally quit your job while still getting paid (the ultimate corporate hack)**

Whether you're a burnt-out manager who's forgotten what joy feels like, an overwhelmed intern who's questioning every life choice that led to this moment, or just someone trying to make it to Friday without committing a workplace felony—this is your handbook for surviving the modern office, one deeply therapeutic eye-roll at a time.

This Isn't Just Venting—It's Strategy

Here's what makes this different from your typical "workplace advice" book: **This actually works.** These aren't theories from someone who's never worked in a cubicle. These are battle-tested strategies from the trenches of corporate America, refined through years of dealing with meeting addicts, credit thieves, and people who think "Reply All" is a form of performance art.

You'll walk away with:

- **Actual scripts** for handling awkward conversations (no more stumbling through confrontations)

- **Email templates** that sound helpful while setting iron-clad boundaries

- **Professional phrases** that translate your rage into HR-approved language

- **Survival tactics** for every type of toxic coworker personality

- **Documentation strategies** that protect your sanity and your career

The Best Part? It's All Completely Legal

Every technique in this book is HR-approved, lawsuit-proof, and professionally bulletproof. You're not learning how to be mean—you're learning how to be strategically kind while protecting your mental health and career prospects.

Because spoiler alert: **It's not you. It's definitely, absolutely, 100% them.**

And now you're going to learn exactly how to deal with "them" without losing your mind, your job, or your carefully maintained professional reputation. Ready to transform from workplace victim to workplace survivor?

Let's figure out how to not just survive, but actually thrive in spite of the people around you.

Warning: By the end of this book, you'll either be promoted for your newfound diplomatic skills, or you'll have enough material to start your own consulting business teaching other people how to deal with impossible coworkers. Both outcomes are acceptable.

CHAPTER ONE

Welcome to Your "Conflict-Free" Workplace (Just Kidding, It's Chaos with Bad Coffee)

You're Not Crazy—They Really Are the Problem

Congratulations! You work in a professional environment where everyone is emotionally mature, communicates clearly, and treats project deadlines like they actually matter.

[Pause for hysterical laughter]

Yeah, right. You work in the real world, where "quick sync" means "prepare to lose an hour of your life you'll never get back," and someone named Brad from Marketing thinks he's revolutionizing business because he discovered the crying-laughing emoji.

Maybe it's the coworker who responds to every Teams message with a thumbs-up instead of an actual answer. Maybe it's the person who schedules meetings called "Touch Base" that somehow become existential crises about the office coffee budget. Or maybe—and hear us out—it's that special teammate who treats "Reply All" like a personal broadcasting network.

This book is for you, the working professional who's trying to maintain some dignity while surrounded by people who think "collaborative brainstorming" means throwing ideas at a wall until someone volunteers to clean up the mess.

Why This Book Exists (Besides The Fact the Therapy is Expensive)

Let's be honest: HR isn't going to save you. They're too busy organizing team-building exercises that cost more than your monthly rent and somehow involve both trust falls and catered sandwiches that taste like cardboard. Your manager is permanently "circling back" on everything like a broken GPS stuck in an endless loop. And if one more person sends you an email saying "Please advise" with zero context, you're going to advise them to find a new career.

You don't need another wellness app telling you to breathe mindfully while your inbox explodes. What you need is a practical guide for surviving the daily madness when your workplace feels like a reality show where everyone forgot the cameras are rolling.

This isn't about changing these people. That's like trying to explain why pineapple doesn't belong on pizza to someone who puts it there anyway—you'll waste your breath, they'll ignore you, and everyone ends up frustrated.

This is about:

- **Surviving without becoming the office villain**
- **Mastering the art of professional diplomacy** (when you'd rather practice professional boxing)
- **Creating paper trails that would make lawyers weep with joy**
- **Saying "Happy to help!" when you'd rather help yourself to the nearest exit**

Who This Book Is For

- Anyone who's become the unofficial tech support because you know how to turn the projector on without calling IT
- People who've been "volunteered" for the committee that plans office birthday parties for people you've never met
- Those who have googled "Is it legal to block your coworker's email address" during their lunch break
- Humans who've said "I'm fine" in meetings while internally writing their resignation letter in haiku form
- Anyone who's had to explain to someone why expecting a reply

WELCOME TO YOUR "CONFLICT-FREE" WORKPLACE... 3

to "urgent" emails on Sunday night is problematic

If you've ever been in a meeting where someone seriously suggested "taking this offline" to discuss where to order lunch from, welcome to the club. We meet at the bar after work and communicate only through eye rolls.

Our Mission (That We're Totally Making Up As We Go)

This survival guide will teach you to:

- **Speak fluent corporate** without losing your soul in the translation
- **Write emails that sound helpful** but are actually masterpieces of professional boundaries
- **Identify workplace red flags** faster than you can delete a meeting invite
- **Set boundaries** without setting fire to your career prospects
- **Keep your sanity** in an environment that seems designed to test it daily

A Brief Word from Fake HR

"At [Insert Your Company Name Here], we're committed to fostering a collaborative environment where everyone's voice is heard, especially the loud ones who interrupt during every presentation. We encourage you to handle workplace challenges through approved channels like this book, strategic coffee breaks, and the ancient art of professional email passive-aggression. Please note that direct confrontation is discouraged, as is anything that might require us to actually manage people."

(Translation: We see the chaos happening. We're not fixing it. Have you tried just dealing with it?)

What You'll Find in These Pages

Each chapter tackles a different flavor of workplace insanity, from the colleague who steals credit faster than office supplies disappear, to the meeting enthusiast who thinks every problem can be solved with more PowerPoint slides and fewer actual solutions.

This survival manual includes:

- **Scripts for those awkward conversations** (because winging it got you into this mess)
- **Email templates** that sound collaborative but feel like diplomatic warfare
- **Workplace personality identification guides** (spoiler: they're all a little broken)
- **Validation that your coworkers really are as unhinged as you think**

Because here's the truth: **It's not you. It's absolutely, scientifically, definitely them.** And we're going to help you navigate their chaos without losing your job, your mind, or your carefully maintained professional reputation.

Ready to transform from workplace victim to workplace survivor? Let's figure out how to succeed in spite of the people around you.

Warning: By the end of this book, you'll either be promoted for your newfound diplomatic skills, or you'll have enough material to write your own workplace comedy special. Both outcomes are acceptable.

CHAPTER TWO

How to Identify the Problem (Spoiler Alert: It's Definitely Not You)

Trust Your Instincts—They Really Are That Difficult

You've tried everything. You've given them every possible benefit of the doubt. You've made excuses: "Maybe they're having a rough week," "Perhaps they don't realize how that sounded," or "Could be they learned communication skills from watching reality TV."

But somewhere deep down, you know the truth: This isn't accidental. This is their actual personality, and they're surprisingly comfortable with it.

Welcome to modern corporate life, where toxic behavior gets rewarded with leadership opportunities and the person who actually does their job gets asked to "be more of a team player" (translation: fix everyone else's mistakes while smiling).

This chapter is your field guide to identifying workplace chaos before it steamrolls your sanity.

You're Not Being Overly Sensitive If...

- Your stress levels spike every time you see their name in your email
- You've developed a physical reaction to the phrase "per my last email"
- You screenshot their messages to send to friends with the caption "Can you believe this?"
- You've found yourself googling "how to professionally tell some-

- one they're crazy"
- You practice saying "That's interesting" in the mirror because it's safer than your real thoughts

Reality check: You're not being dramatic. You're being human in an increasingly inhumane work environment.

The Corporate Red Flag Collection

Check these off when you spot them in the wild:

The Credit Thief: Takes ownership of group accomplishments and presents them as personal victories in meetings

The Crisis Creator: Manufactures emergencies from situations that could have been prevented with basic planning

The Memory Eraser: "I never said that" (you have the email), "That's not what I meant" (it's literally what they wrote)

The Professional Contrarian: Responds to "The building is on fire" with "Well, let me play devil's advocate here..."

The Buzzword Generator: Speaks exclusively in LinkedIn-post language and thinks "synergistic optimization" is a real skill

The Fake Visionary: Calls themselves a "big picture thinker" but their biggest innovation is color-coding their task lists

The Brutal Honesty Enthusiast: "I'm just being direct" is their motto, "I'm just being mean" is the translation

If you've checked more than three boxes, congratulations! You're not in a normal workplace—you're in a behavioral psychology experiment testing how much nonsense one person can endure before they start updating their resume.

Early Warning System: Spotting Trouble Before It Finds You

Some problematic behaviors are subtle. Others are about as discreet as a fire drill. Here's your identification guide:

HOW TO IDENTIFY THE PROBLEM (SPOILER ALERT: IT'S...

The Stealth Problems

The Concern Troll: "I'm just worried about your workload" when you set reasonable boundaries, as if having limits is a character flaw.

The Compliment Assassin: "You're so good at [minor task], not like [important thing you actually excel at], but really great at [completely unrelated minor thing]!"

The Two-Faced Teammate: Agrees with you privately, contradicts you publicly, then acts confused when you're not thrilled about it.

The Obvious Chaos Agents

The Reply-All Bomber: Uses company-wide emails as their personal blog. Recent subject line: "RE: RE: RE: Coffee machine update and my thoughts on office temperature"

The Meeting Hostage-Taker: Schedules 30-minute check-ins that become 90-minute therapy sessions about their strategic vision for the supply closet.

The Oversharing Specialist: Thinks team meetings are group therapy and the work chat is their personal diary.

Your Sanity Checkpoint

When you start questioning your own judgment, remember these facts:

- **"Their inability to communicate clearly isn't your job to try to decode."**
- **"Professional courtesy has limits, and they've found them."**
- **"Setting boundaries isn't having an attitude problem."**
- **"Their poor planning doesn't automatically become your emergency."**
- **"You can be helpful without being taken advantage of."**

The Scientific Method: Testing Your Theory

Still not sure if they're the problem? Try this experiment:

1. **Document everything** for one week. Screenshots, email timestamps, witness accounts.

2. **Show the evidence** to a trusted friend or family member without context.

3. **Watch their reaction.** If they start laughing or look horrified, you have your answer.

Final Reality Check

You're not imagining things. You're not being too sensitive. You're definitely not the problem.

You're a reasonably functional adult trying to work with people who learned their professional skills from reality TV and their management techniques from medieval warfare manuals.

Now that we've established you're not losing your mind, let's learn how to handle the madness around you—with grace, professionalism, and just enough strategic thinking to keep things interesting.

The good news? Once you can identify the chaos, you can start navigating it. Or at least document it well enough for really entertaining stories later.

Up Next: Chapter 3 – HR-Approved Phrases for Handling Coworkers Who Suck

Learn the sacred art of saying "Back off" with a smile and a passive-aggressive font choice.

CHAPTER THREE

HR-Approved Phrases for Handling Coworkers Who Suck

How to Say "You're the Worst" Without Becoming Newly Unemployed

Some people make you want to throw your laptop into the void and become a hermit who sells artisanal candles on Etsy. But alas, you need that health insurance and the ability to afford groceries that aren't ramen.

So how do you tell someone they're absolutely unhinged when corporate wants you to "maintain a positive workplace culture" and your manager thinks conflict resolution means forwarding you a motivational article about teamwork?

You master the delicate art of the Professionally Savage Email—phrases so politely brutal they could be taught in business school as advanced diplomacy.

The Corporate Translation Dictionary

These phrases sound helpful but pack the emotional punch of a passive-aggressive greeting card.

"Just circling back on this!" *What it really means:* I sent this email three times and you're ignoring me harder than a telemarketer. I will continue haunting your inbox until you respond or change jobs.

"Per my last email..." *What it really means:* I literally just explained this with the thoroughness of a Wikipedia article, and yet here we are again, like we're trapped in some corporate version of Groundhog Day.

10   HR APPROVED WAYS TO DEAL WITH STUPID COWORKERS

"Let's schedule a quick call to align!" *What it really means:* You're being deliberately dense via text and I need to see your face when I explain this like you're a confused golden retriever.

"I love the enthusiasm!" *What it really means:* That idea is completely insane and I'm genuinely impressed by your confidence in presenting it.

"Thanks for bringing this to my attention!" *What it really means:* You just told me something I already knew, but please, continue explaining my own job to me.

"Let's take a step back here..." *What it really means:* You're spiraling faster than an F5 tornado and I need to reality-check this situation.

Sample Emails That Hit Different

Scenario: Derek from Sales took credit for your entire marketing campaign in front of the CEO.

Subject: Quick Note on Campaign Development

Hi Derek!

Thanks for presenting the Q3 campaign results today! Your enthusiasm really came through. I wanted to make sure we capture the full development story for our records, since this project had quite a journey.

As you mentioned, this was definitely a collaborative effort. The initial strategy framework and creative direction were developed by our team back in July (I've attached the original proposal for reference). It's been great seeing how the campaign evolved from concept to execution.

For future presentations, it might be helpful to include a brief overview of the development timeline and list of participants so everyone gets the full picture of the extensive teamwork involved.

Looking forward to our continued collaboration!

Best, [Your Name]

P.S. I've cc'd Sarah from Marketing to help update our project documentation accordingly.

(Translation: I have receipts, Derek. Try that credit-stealing nonsense again and I'll expose you faster than a data breach.)

Scenario: Linda keeps scheduling "urgent" meetings that could have been handled with a two-sentence email.

Subject: Streamlining Our Communication

Hi Linda!

I've been thinking about how we can optimize our collaboration process. I noticed we've been jumping on a lot of calls lately, and I'm wondering if we could experiment with handling some of our quick check-ins asynchronously?

I'm trying to block out some focused work time this week for the big projects, so I'd love to see if we can use email or Teams for the day-to-day updates and save our meeting time for the strategic discussions that really benefit from face-to-face brainstorming.

What do you think? Happy to discuss the best approach!

[Your Name]

(Translation: Linda, I'm begging you to stop treating my calendar like your personal entertainment system. Not everything needs a meeting, especially at 4:30 PM on Friday.)

Phrases to Avoid (Unless You Want an HR Meeting)

- "Are you serious right now?" *(Too honest)*
- "That makes zero sense." *(Accurate but career-limiting)*
- "Did anyone actually think this through?" *(Valid question, wrong audience)*
- "This is why we can't have nice things." *(Save it for your group chat)*
- "I'm not paid enough for this nonsense." *(True, but keep it to yourself)*

These may feel therapeutic in the moment, but HR has excellent hearing and a surprisingly good memory for workplace drama.

Advanced Professional Warfare Moves

The Strategic Documentation: Follow up every bizarre conversation with an email: "Thanks for the chat! Just wanted to confirm we discussed [exactly what they said]..."

The Polite Redirect: When they try to dump their work on you: "I'd love to help, but I'm at capacity with [important-sounding project]. Have you considered [literally anyone else]?"

The Concerned Colleague: "I noticed [problem] has been happening frequently. Should we flag this for [their boss] to see if there's additional support available?"

The Calendar Shield: Block your schedule with "Deep Work" or "Strategic Planning" when you see them approaching with that "got a minute?" look.

Your Professional Survival Kit

Keep these tactics in your back pocket:

1. **Respond, don't react.** Take a deep breath, maybe eat a snack, then craft your response like the diplomatic genius you are.

2. **Use the 24-hour rule.** For especially infuriating emails, write your response immediately, then delete it and write a professional version the next day.

3. **Master the art of strategic CCing.** Every email should serve a purpose beyond just covering your own behind.

4. **Document everything.** Screenshots, email timestamps, meeting notes. Build your case like you're preparing for corporate court.

5. **Find your workplace allies.** Identify the other sane people and stick together. Shared suffering builds the strongest bonds.

The Ultimate Power Move: Strategic Silence

Sometimes the most devastating response is a carefully timed non-response. Read their ridiculous request, consider it thoughtfully, and then... just don't reply immediately. Let them wonder if their email disappeared into the digital void.

When you finally respond 2-3 business days later, offer something on your own terms:

"Hi! Thanks for your patience—things have been absolutely swamped over here! Yes, I can help with [reasonable version of their unreasonable request]. Let me know if that works for you."

It's the professional equivalent of "Sorry, my phone was on silent" and it works every time.

Coming Up Next: Chapter 4 – Workplace Species: A Field Guide to Office Creatures

From the Meeting Monger who hoards your calendar time to the Credit Pirate who raids your accomplishments—learn to identify and survive every type of workplace predator.

Chapter Four

Workplace Species: A Field Guide to Office Creatures

Know Your Ecosystem (And How to Survive It)

Every workplace is essentially a nature preserve for the professionally bizarre. Some species are harmless (like the Plant Parent who talks to the office ficus), some are mildly irritating (like the Microwave Fish Enthusiast), and some are genuinely dangerous to your mental health and career progression.

This chapter is your survival guide to identifying and managing the most toxic workplace creatures before they can drain your sanity and steal your lunch from the break room fridge.

Level 1 Threats: Annoying But Manageable

The Reply-All Enthusiast

Habitat: Every single email thread, whether they belong there or not.

Behavior: Responds "Thanks!" to company-wide announcements about policy changes. Says "Please remove me" from optional newsletters they personally signed up for. Once started a 73-email chain by reply-all wishing someone happy birthday.

Survival Strategy:

- Use email filters like your life depends on it
- Master the "mute conversation" function
- Start a separate group chat called "Survivors of the Reply-All Apocalypse"

Threat Level: Mild annoyance that makes you question human evolution

The Video Call Disaster Magnet

Habitat: Every Zoom meeting, where they're always having "technical difficulties."

Behavior: Joins meetings late because they can't find the link. Uses virtual backgrounds that make them look like a floating head in the Bahamas. Somehow always eating crunchy snacks during presentations.

Survival Strategy:

- Perfect your "Oh, your mic is muted" poker face
- Keep a running tally of their tech failures for entertainment
- Always have a backup plan that doesn't involve their participation

Threat Level: Comic relief with occasional productivity casualties

Level 2 Threats: Moderately Dangerous

The Credit Pirate

Habitat: Lurks around successful projects, waiting to claim treasure.

Behavior: Uses phrases like "As I was saying..." to introduce ideas they heard you present five minutes ago. Shows up to present work they've never seen before. Has perfected the art of being in the right Teams channel at exactly the right moment.

Survival Strategy:

- Document everything with timestamps (screenshots are your best friend)
- Use phrases like "Building on the framework I developed..."
- Send follow-up emails after every conversation: "Great discussion! Just to confirm what I proposed..."

Threat Level: Career-limiting if not addressed quickly

The Meeting Monger

Habitat: Your calendar, which they treat like their personal scheduling playground.

Behavior: Sends invites for "quick 15-minute catch-ups" that become hour-long therapy sessions. Creates meetings to plan meetings. Genuinely believes every human interaction should be scheduled, recorded, and followed up with action items.

Survival Strategy:

- Always ask "What's the agenda?" before accepting any meeting
- Suggest alternatives: "Could we handle this in email first?"
- Block your calendar for "project work" before they can claim it

Threat Level: Soul-crushing productivity drain

Level 3 Threats: Actively Hostile

The Office Therapist

Habitat: Wherever there's drama or someone having a normal human emotion.

Behavior: Turns every casual conversation into a deep dive into your personal life. Shares way too much information about their weekend, their relationships, and their thoughts on your haircut. Makes your good news about their problems somehow.

Survival Strategy:

- Master the subject change: "Speaking of challenges, how about those quarterly numbers?"
- Set clear boundaries: "I'm pretty focused on work stuff today, but thanks for checking in!"
- Develop selective hearing for anything starting with "My thera-

pist says..."

Threat Level: Emotional exhaustion that spreads like office flu

The Workplace Gaslighter

Habitat: Everywhere, rewriting reality in real-time.

Behavior: "I never said that" (you have the email thread). "We all agreed on this approach" (literally no one agreed). "I think there's been a misunderstanding" (the only misunderstanding is their relationship with the truth).

Survival Strategy:

- Document every interaction in writing
- Use phrases like "Just to confirm our conversation..."
- Trust your memory and your email history
- Keep witnesses when possible

Threat Level: Sanity-threatening, reputation-damaging if unchecked

Boss Level Threats: Proceed with Extreme Caution

The Micromanager Maniac

Habitat: Your desk, your inbox, your peripheral vision at all times.

Behavior: Asks for updates on projects you started twenty minutes ago. Wants to review your emails before you send them. Schedules daily check-ins to discuss your bathroom break schedule (not really, but almost).

Survival Strategy:

- Over-communicate proactively to reduce their anxiety
- Set clear expectations: "I'll have an update for you by Friday at 2 PM"

- Document their unreasonable requests (for your own sanity)

Threat Level: Complete autonomy annihilation

The Toxic Positivity Pusher

Habitat: Wherever someone dares to express a normal human emotion like frustration or concern.

Behavior: Responds to legitimate workplace complaints with "But look on the bright side!" Suggests yoga for systemic organizational problems. Believes every issue can be solved with gratitude journaling and essential oils.

Survival Strategy:

- Validate your own feelings privately
- Respond with facts: "The system actually needs to be fixed, not embraced"
- Find allies who understand that sometimes things genuinely suck

Threat Level: Reality distortion that can make you question your own sanity

Survival Tactics for the Office Ecosystem

The Golden Rules:

1. **Don't feed the energy vampires.** Engaging with their chaos only makes them stronger and hungrier.

2. **Document like a nature photographer.** Screenshots, timestamps, witness statements. Build your evidence portfolio.

3. **Find your tribe.** Identify the normal humans and form alliances. Group chat solidarity is real and powerful.

4. **Practice the gray rock method.** Be polite but boring. Don't give them material to work with.

5. **Remember: You're not trying to change them.** You're just trying to survive them with your dignity intact.

Emergency Protocols:

- Keep a "What Even Is This" folder for particularly unhinged interactions
- Rate your coworkers on a 1-10 chaos scale (for your own entertainment)
- Develop exit strategies for every type of conversation
- Practice your professional responses so you don't accidentally say what you're really thinking

Remember: You can't control the insanity, but you can absolutely control how you respond to it. Stay hydrated, keep your headphones charged, and never underestimate the power of a well-timed bathroom break to escape a toxic interaction.

Coming Up Next: Chapter 5 – How to Write a Complaint So Good, HR Will Frame It

Master the art of professional documentation that's so clear, so reasonable, and so ironclad that even HR can't ignore it. Think of it as creative writing, but with legal implications.

Chapter Five

How to Write a Complaint So Good, HR Will Frame It

The Art of Professional Revenge Through Perfect Documentation

Sometimes, being the bigger person just means writing a much better email. Whether you're documenting chaos, whistleblowing with style, or building an airtight case for why your coworker should be launched into the sun, this chapter will teach you how to weaponize professionalism.

This isn't about venting your frustrations into the digital void. This is about crafting a masterpiece of corporate communication—the kind of email that makes HR pause their lunch, nod slowly, and say, "Well, this is awkward... for everyone except the person who wrote this."

The Key Ingredients of Complaint Gold

1. Tone So Professional It Hurts: No insults, no sarcasm (that they can prove), and definitely no emojis—unless it's a single smiley face, deployed strategically like a sniper.

2. Facts Colder Than Your Office's Air Conditioning: Include dates, times, witnesses, and exact quotes. Write like you're producing a documentary series called "When Workplace Behavior Goes Wrong."

3. Emotional Detachment Worthy of a Zen Master: Feel all the rage, but write like you're made of spreadsheets and herbal tea.

4. Include Solutions That Make You Look Like a Team Player: Because HR doesn't want to solve problems—they want you to solve problems while they update their LinkedIn profiles.

22 HR APPROVED WAYS TO DEAL WITH STUPID COWORKERS

Sample Email: The Perfect Professional Takedown

Scenario: Marcus from IT has been "too busy" to fix your computer for three weeks, but somehow has time to play online chess during meetings.

Subject: IT Support Follow-Up - Workstation Issues

Hi [HR Manager] and [IT Director],

I wanted to document a recurring support issue that's impacting my ability to meet project deadlines. Over the past three weeks, I've submitted multiple tickets regarding my workstation's performance issues (Ticket #4721, #4856, #4901).

Timeline of events:

- April 3: Initial ticket submitted, acknowledged same day
- April 10: Follow-up meeting scheduled, postponed by IT
- April 17: Escalation requested, meeting rescheduled
- April 24: Third attempt at resolution, no follow-through

During our team meeting yesterday, I observed that other technical projects are progressing normally, so I understand the IT team has capacity for urgent items. I'm hoping we can prioritize this issue since it's affecting the Q2 deliverables that depend on my workstation functionality.

I'm happy to coordinate with any alternative IT support or discuss temporary solutions that would help maintain productivity while we resolve this.

Looking forward to a swift resolution.

Best regards,[Your Name]

(Translation: Marcus plays chess while my computer crashes, I have proof, and now everyone including his boss knows about it. Fix this or explain to the CEO why Q2 is delayed because of online games.)

The Art of the Devastating P.S.

Never underestimate the power of a perfectly placed postscript:

- *"P.S. I've attached screenshots of the error messages for reference."* (And Marcus's chess game in the background)
- *"P.S. Happy to provide additional context in a brief meeting."* (Where I will destroy you with facts)
- *"P.S. I've copied the project team for visibility on timeline impacts."* (Your reputation is now everyone's business)

Phrases That Sound Helpful But Are Actually Weapons

"I wanted to ensure this was properly documented..." *Translation: This is going in your permanent record.*

"To help provide context for future planning..." *Translation: So this never happens again, to anyone, ever.*

"I'm confident this was an oversight..." *Translation: Prove me wrong, I dare you.*

"Looking forward to your guidance on next steps..." *Translation: Fix this or explain why you can't to people who matter.*

The Complaint Quality Checklist

Before hitting send, make sure you can check every box:

- **Did you include specific dates and times?**
- **Did you avoid emotional language?**
- **Did you offer solutions, not just problems?**
- **Did you copy the right people (but not too many people)?**
- **Would this email make sense to someone who knows nothing about the situation?**
- **Could this be read aloud in court without embarrassing**

you?

If you answered "yes" to all of the above, congratulations. You've created a document so professionally devastating it could be used as evidence in workplace efficiency trials.

Advanced Complaint Techniques

The Innocent Question Technique: "I'm hoping you can help clarify the company policy on [thing they obviously violated]..."

The Concerned Colleague Approach: "I noticed [person] seemed overwhelmed lately. Should we discuss additional support resources?"

The Process Improvement Angle: "This situation highlighted some opportunities to strengthen our workflow. I've drafted some suggestions..."

What NOT to Include (Even If It's True)

- "This is ridiculous"
- "I can't believe I have to explain this"
- "Anyone with half a brain would know..."
- "This is the stupidest thing I've ever seen"
- Screenshots of their social media posts during work hours (tempting, but illegal)

Save these thoughts for your group chat, where they belong.

The Golden Rule of Professional Complaints

Make it impossible for them to ignore you without looking incompetent themselves.

HR doesn't care about your feelings. They care about liability, productivity, and avoiding awkward conversations with executives. Give them documentation so clean, so reasonable, and so obviously correct that addressing the problem becomes easier than explaining why they didn't.

Coming Up Next: Chapter 6 – Passive-Aggressive Communication Styles Ranked from "Mildly Petty" to "Requires Intervention"

A comprehensive guide to workplace passive-aggression, from the gentle art of the delayed email response to the nuclear option of cc'ing someone's mother (metaphorically speaking).

Chapter Six

Passive-Aggressive Communication Styles Ranked from "Mildly Petty" to "Requires Intervention"

Because Sometimes Silence Speaks Louder Than Words

Passive-aggression is the unofficial language of corporate America—we all speak it, we all understand it, and we all pretend we don't know what it means when HR asks. From the weaponized "per my last email" to the devastating art of reading receipts without responses, this chapter explores the beautiful spectrum of professional pettiness.

Let's rank the most common forms of workplace passive-aggression, from harmless office theater to behavior that might require a wellness check.

Level 1: Mildly Annoying (Amateur Hour)

1. **"Thanks for your patience..."** *When they weren't patient at all*
Pettiness Level: 2/10
Professional Risk: None
Translation: I know you're annoyed, and I'm acknowledging it without apologizing.

2. **"Just following up on this!"** *The fourth follow-up in two days*
Pettiness Level: 3/10
Professional Risk: Low
Translation: You're ignoring me and we both know it.

3. **Responding "Noted." to lengthy emails**
Pettiness Level: 4/10
Professional Risk: Low
Translation: I read your novel. I'm not impressed.

Level 2: Professionally Petty (Getting Warmer)

4. "Per my last email..." followed by copy-pasting the exact same text
Pettiness Level: 5/10
Professional Risk: Moderate (if overused)
Translation: Learn to read or learn to suffer.

5. Setting read receipts on, then not responding for days
Pettiness Level: 6/10
Professional Risk: Moderate
Translation: I saw your message. I'm choosing chaos.

6. "Let's take this offline" in front of the entire team
Pettiness Level: 6/10
Professional Risk: Moderate
Translation: You're embarrassing yourself publicly, and I'm giving you one chance to stop.

Level 3: Advanced Workplace Warfare (Things Are Getting Spicy)

7. Scheduling a meeting titled "Quick Chat" with no agenda or context
Pettiness Level: 7/10
Professional Risk: High if they're senior to you
Translation: You'll spend the weekend wondering what you did wrong.

8. "Happy to clarify!" followed by an explanation that's somehow more confusing
Pettiness Level: 7/10
Professional Risk: High
Translation: You're either stupid or pretending to be stupid, and either way, I'm here for it.

9. "Adding [boss's name] for visibility"
Pettiness Level: 8/10
Professional Risk: Very High
Translation: I'm escalating this nuclear-style and your reputation is collateral damage.

Level 4: Nuclear Option (Proceed with Extreme Caution)

10. "I'll let you handle this since you seem to have strong opinions about the approach"
Pettiness Level: 9/10
Professional Risk: Extremely High
Translation: Congratulations, you just inherited all responsibility for this disaster.

11. Sending a calendar invite for "Project Retrospective" after something goes wrong
Pettiness Level: 9/10
Professional Risk: Career-limiting
Translation: We're going to discuss your failures in a formal, documented setting.

12. "Thanks for your feedback. I'll take it under advisement." *When the feedback was actually a direct order*
Pettiness Level: 10/10
Professional Risk: You might need to update your resume
Translation: I hear you talking, but I don't hear you managing me.

Honorable Mentions: Special Categories

The Delayed Response Power Play
Waiting exactly long enough to respond that they know it was intentional, but not so long that it's unprofessional. A+ for timing.

The Strategic Typo
"Dear Mr. Smith" when their name is clearly "Schmidt" in their email signature. Plausible deniability with maximum insult.

The Meeting Inception
Scheduling a meeting to discuss scheduling another meeting. Peak corporate absurdity.

The Malicious Compliance Special
Doing exactly what they asked for, nothing more, nothing less, watching it fail spectacularly, then saying "I followed your instructions exactly."

How to Respond Without Becoming the Villain

Mirror their energy, but dial it down one level:

- Them: "Per my last email..."
- You: "Thanks for the reminder! Let me address that now."

Use humor to deflate the tension:

- "Looks like we've got a fun game of inbox tag going—let me close the loop on this."

Go full ice queen professional:

- "I appreciate the follow-up. I'll prioritize this accordingly."

Final Thought

Passive-aggression is like office caffeine—a little bit can be energizing and even helpful for getting things done. Too much, and everyone starts getting jittery and making poor decisions.

Use these powers responsibly. The goal isn't to win the passive-aggressive Olympics; it's to survive the workplace with your sanity and your reputation intact. Sometimes that means being sweetly, professionally brutal. Sometimes it means being the bigger person who actually addresses issues directly.

Choose your battles wisely, and remember: the best passive-aggressive move is often the one you don't make.

Coming Up Next: Chapter 7 – Conflict Role Play: How to "Address Issues Directly" Without Having a Nervous Breakdown

Because sometimes your manager, HR, or that one overly optimistic colleague will suggest you "just talk to them directly," and you'll need a survival plan.

CHAPTER SEVEN

Conflict Role Play: How to Address Issues Directly Without Having a Nervous Breakdown

When Someone Suggests You "Just Talk to Them"

At some point, someone will utter the dreaded phrase: "Have you tried addressing this directly with them?" And you'll want to respond with, "Have you tried jumping out of a plane without a parachute?" But instead, you'll smile and nod because you're a professional.

This chapter is your survival guide for those moments when avoiding the problem is no longer an option, and you actually have to look your difficult coworker in the eye and have A Conversation.

Why Direct Confrontation Feels Like Extreme Sports

Direct workplace conversations are terrifying because:

- **They're emotionally loaded** (three weeks of built-up frustration tends to do that)
- **There's usually an audience** (even if it's just the office fern, someone will hear about it)
- **You're expected to be "professional"** (whatever that means when someone has been sabotaging your projects)
- **There's no undo button** (you can't unsay what you've said, no matter how much you wish you could)

But here's the thing: with the right approach, you can have these conversations without losing your mind, your job, or your ability to make eye contact at the coffee machine.

Role Play Scenario 1: The Credit Thief

What happened: Jennifer took credit for your entire presentation in front of the board.

What you want to say: "You presentation-stealing, spotlight-hogging, credit-snatching piranha!"

What you should say: "Hi Jennifer. I wanted to follow up on yesterday's board meeting. I noticed you presented the client retention strategy without mentioning the team contributions. I'd like to make sure we're aligned on how we represent collaborative work going forward."

Why it works:

- Uses "I noticed" (calm observer, not accuser)
- Mentions "team contributions" (collaborative, not just about you)
- Asks for future alignment (solution-focused)
- No name-calling (surprisingly)

Role Play Scenario 2: The Meeting Hijacker

What happened: Dave turns every 15-minute check-in into a 45-minute therapy session about his weekend plans.

What you want to say: "Dave, I don't care about your cat's dental surgery or your mother-in-law's opinions about your kitchen renovation!"

What you should say: "Dave, I want to make sure we're making the best use of our time in these check-ins. I've got about 15 minutes to focus on the project updates. Should we create a separate time to catch up on other things?"

Why it works:

- Focuses on time management, not personality
- Acknowledges his need to chat without encouraging it

- Offers an alternative that you'll never actually schedule

Role Play Scenario 3: The Deadline Dodger

What happened: Marcus consistently misses deadlines, making you look bad to clients.

What you want to say: "You don't just miss deadlines. You assassinate them and bury the evidence."

What you should say: "Marcus, I've noticed we've had some timing challenges on the last few projects. The client deliverables depend on your pieces being ready when we discussed. Can we walk through your process to see if there are any blockers I can help address?"

Why it works:

- "Timing challenges" sounds less personal than "you're always late"
- Mentions client impact (adds external pressure)
- Offers help rather than just criticism
- Requests process discussion (collaborative problem-solving)

Your Conflict Conversation Toolkit

Phrases to Use:

- "I want to make sure we're aligned..."
- "I've noticed [behavior] and wanted to understand..."
- "Can we discuss how to handle [situation] going forward?"
- "I want to find a solution that works for everyone..."

Phrases to Avoid:

- "You always..." or "You never..."
- "That's just how you are"

- "Not to be rude, but..." (you're about to be rude)
- "Everyone thinks..." (don't drag others into your mess)

The Pre-Conversation Prep Checklist

Before you open your mouth:

Practice in the mirror (yes, really—it helps you hear how you sound)

Write down your main points (so you don't get derailed by their deflections)

Choose your timing (not right before lunch, not during their busiest day)

Pick a private location (conference rooms, not the break room)

Have a backup plan (if they get defensive, how will you exit gracefully?)

How to Tell If It's Going Well

Good signs:

- They're asking questions instead of making excuses
- They acknowledge your perspective ("I can see how that would be frustrating")
- They suggest solutions or ask what would help
- The conversation stays focused on behavior, not personality

Warning signs:

- They start bringing up your past mistakes
- They get defensive and personal
- They refuse to acknowledge there's even a problem
- They try to turn it into a discussion about your attitude

Exit Strategies for When It Goes Sideways

If they get hostile: "I can see this is a sensitive topic. Let's take some time to think about it and revisit when we can focus on solutions."

If they play the victim: "I understand this feedback might be surprising. The important thing is figuring out how we move forward effectively."

If they completely shut down: "I appreciate you listening. I'll send a brief follow-up email so we're both clear on next steps."

The Post-Conversation Follow-Up

Always, always, always send a follow-up email:

Subject: Follow-up on our conversation

Hi [Name],

Thanks for taking the time to discuss [issue] with me today. I wanted to summarize what we talked about to make sure we're on the same page:

- [Main point 1]
- [Main point 2]
- [Agreed-upon solution or next steps]

I'm looking forward to working together on this. Let me know if you have any questions or if I missed anything.

Best, [Your Name]

Why this matters: It documents the conversation, prevents "I never said that" situations later, and shows you're serious about following through.

Success Metrics

You know the conversation was successful if:

- You didn't cry, scream, or threaten anyone

- You said what you needed to say
- They didn't storm off or report you to HR
- You have a clear next step or agreement
- You can still function in the same office without hiding in the supply closet

Remember: the goal isn't to become best friends or fix their entire personality. The goal is to address the specific issue so you can do your job without losing your mind.

Coming Up Next: Chapter 8 – Performance Review Prep: How to Spin "I Survived This Year" into "Exceeds Expectations"

Because "showed up consistently and didn't quit" is actually a significant achievement that deserves recognition, and we're going to help you articulate that professionally.

CHAPTER EIGHT

Performance Review Prep: How to Spin "I Survived This Year" into "Exceeds Expectations"

The Art of Professional Self-Promotion for People Who Hate Talking About Themselves

Performance review season: that magical time of year when you have to pretend that updating spreadsheets and surviving daily chaos constitutes "strategic leadership" and "innovative problem-solving", and when modest people become corporate poets, and introverts transform into personal brand marketers.

Here's your guide to turning everyday workplace survival into performance review gold, without sounding like a motivational LinkedIn post that makes people unfollow you.

The Corporate Achievement Translation Machine

What You Actually Did: Responded to emails
Performance Review Version: "Maintained consistent communication channels, ensuring stakeholder alignment and project continuity"

What You Actually Did: Fixed the printer for the 27th time
Performance Review Version: "Provided technical leadership and operational support, reducing downtime and optimizing team productivity"

What You Actually Did: Didn't quit when everything went wrong
Performance Review Version: "Demonstrated resilience and adaptability during organizational transitions, maintaining performance standards under challenging conditions"

What You Actually Did: Explained the same thing to five different people

Performance Review Version: "Facilitated knowledge transfer across diverse stakeholder groups, ensuring consistent understanding and implementation"

The Universal Performance Review Buzz Phrase Generator

Pick one from each category and combine for instant achievement:

Action Verbs:

- Spearheaded
- Optimized
- Streamlined
- Facilitated
- Enhanced
- Implemented

Buzzword Bridges:

- cross-functional collaboration
- process improvements
- stakeholder engagement
- strategic initiatives
- operational efficiency
- client satisfaction

Impact Statements:

- resulting in increased productivity
- leading to improved outcomes
- driving measurable results

PERFORMANCE REVIEW PREP: HOW TO SPIN "I SURVIVED...   41

- supporting organizational goals
- enhancing team performance
- exceeding expectations

Example: "Spearheaded cross-functional collaboration, resulting in increased productivity and enhanced team performance."

Translation: I attended meetings and answered emails like a functional adult.

Actual Examples of Professional Spin

Scenario: You spent three months dealing with a difficult client who changed their mind constantly.

Don't Write: "Client was indecisive and drove me insane"

Do Write: "Successfully managed complex client relationship through multiple project iterations, demonstrating flexibility and solution-oriented approach while maintaining project timelines and budget parameters. Developed enhanced change management protocols that improved client satisfaction scores."

Scenario: You trained the new hire who asked 400 questions per day.

Don't Write: "Babysat the new person because they couldn't figure out basic tasks"

Do Write: "Led comprehensive onboarding and mentorship program for new team member, developing customized training materials and providing ongoing support. Created knowledge-sharing framework that reduced onboarding time and improved new hire integration success."

Scenario: You fixed a problem that should never have been your responsibility.

Don't Write: "Cleaned up someone else's mess because they were incompetent"

Do Write: "Identified critical process gap and implemented rapid solution, preventing potential client impact. Collaborated across departments to develop sustainable prevention strategies and improved workflow documentation."

Words That Make Everything Sound More Important

Instead of "helped", use "facilitated," "enabled," or "supported"
Instead of "worked on", use "led," "managed," or "oversaw"
Instead of "did", use "executed," "delivered," or "achieved"
Instead of "talked to", use "collaborated with," "partnered with," or "engaged"

The Numbers Game: Quantifying the Unquantifiable

Even if your job doesn't involve obvious metrics, you can find numbers:

- "Processed 150+ client communications weekly"
- "Maintained 99% project delivery rate"
- "Reduced response time by 50%" (from 2 hours to 1 hour)
- "Supported 12 concurrent projects"
- "Achieved 100% training completion rate"
- "Managed relationships with 25+ stakeholders"

Pro tip: If you can't find impressive numbers, create impressive percentages. "Improved process efficiency" sounds better as "Achieved 30% improvement in process efficiency."

What NOT to Include (Even If It's True)

- "Survived despite management decisions"
- "Prevented complete disaster through personal intervention"
- "Maintained sanity against all odds"
- "Exceeded expectations considering the circumstances"

- "Achieved results without adequate resources or support"

Save these honest assessments for your diary or your therapist.

Sample Self-Evaluation: Before and After

BEFORE (Honest Version): *This year was a hot mess. I spent most of my time putting out fires that other people started, dealing with unrealistic deadlines, and trying to make sense of constantly changing priorities. I managed not to have a nervous breakdown, which I consider a major achievement. I also helped train Sarah, who asked me the same questions 27 times but eventually figured it out.*

AFTER (Performance Review Version): *This year I demonstrated exceptional adaptability and problem-solving capabilities in a dynamic environment. I successfully managed multiple high-priority initiatives while maintaining quality standards and meeting aggressive timelines. Key achievements include implementing crisis management protocols that prevented potential client impacts, and developing a comprehensive training program that improved new team member integration. I consistently exceeded delivery expectations while supporting organizational transition initiatives and contributing to team development goals.*

The Art of the Humble Brag

Frame your achievements in terms of team success:

- "I was fortunate to contribute to..."
- "Working with the team, we were able to..."
- "Through collaborative efforts, I helped achieve..."

This makes you sound like a team player rather than someone who thinks they're the office superhero.

Preparing for the Actual Conversation

What they'll ask: "What are you most proud of this year?"
What to say: Pick your strongest quantified achievement and tell a brief story with a clear beginning, middle, and result.

What they'll ask: "What areas would you like to develop?"
What to say: Choose something that sounds like growth, not weakness. "I'd love to develop my strategic planning skills" not "I'm terrible at long-term thinking."

What they'll ask: "Where do you see yourself in a year?"
What to say: Something that benefits them. "Contributing at a higher strategic level" not "Getting the hell out of here."

Final Thoughts

Remember: Performance reviews aren't about honesty—they're about translation. You're not lying about your accomplishments; you're presenting them in the language your company understands and values.

You survived another year in corporate America. You showed up, did the work, solved problems, and helped other people succeed. That deserves recognition, even if you have to write it in business-speak to get it.

Coming Up Next: Chapter 9 – Meetings That Could've Been Emails and Other Crimes Against Productivity

A comprehensive guide to surviving, avoiding, and occasionally weaponizing the modern meeting culture that's somehow convinced us that talking about work is the same as doing work.

CHAPTER NINE

Meetings That Could've Been Emails and Other Crimes Against Productivity

Your Calendar Is Not a War Crime, But It's Close

Welcome to the modern workplace, where time is money, and yet every Tuesday at 2 PM, someone insists on spending both in a virtual room discussing the logistics of discussing logistics.

If you've ever spent more time in meetings than actually working... if you've stared at a 12-person invite wondering what the meeting is about... if you've left a "Daily Standup" feeling like you need to lie down—then you may be a victim of calendar abuse.

Common Meeting Offenses Ranked by Emotional Damage

The "Status Update" Circle of Death: Everyone takes turns saying "no updates" for 45 minutes while your coffee goes cold and your soul leaves your body.
Damage Level: 3/10 (mostly just boring)
Suggested Action: Master the art of looking engaged while mentally planning your grocery list.

The "Quick Sync" That Lasts Forever: Scheduled for 15 minutes. Actual duration: 73 minutes of your life you'll never get back.
Damage Level: 6/10 (time theft)
Suggested Action: "I have a hard stop at [original end time]" and stick to it like your sanity depends on it.

The "All-Hands" Information Dump: Could have been an email. Should have been an email. Will definitely be summarized in an email afterward.
Damage Level: 4/10 (inefficient but survivable)

Suggested Action: Perfect your "actively listening" face while catching up on actual work.

The "Brainstorming Session" Without Parameters: "Let's think outside the box!" they say, then shoot down every creative idea because it doesn't fit in their very specific, unmentioned box.
Damage Level: 8/10 (creativity crusher)
Suggested Action: Ask "What are we optimizing for?" and watch them scramble.

The Friday 4:30 PM "Emergency" Meeting: This is either incompetence or psychological warfare. Possibly both.
Damage Level: 10/10 (crime against humanity)
Suggested Action: "I'll need to join from my car" and then don't. You're already mentally checked out anyway.

Types of People Who Should Not Be Allowed to Schedule Meetings

- **The Rambler** Needs 45 minutes to make a 3-minute point. Thinks silence is a personal attack on their existence.

- **The Vague Scheduler** Sends calendar invites titled "Catch Up" with no context, no agenda, and no mercy for your anxiety levels.

- **The Meeting Inception Specialist** Schedules meetings to plan other meetings. Their calendar looks like a game of Tetris designed by someone having a breakdown.

- **The Hostage Taker** Keeps everyone 20 minutes past the scheduled end time because "we're making such good progress" (translation: I don't want to do actual work).

- **The Over-Includer** Invites the entire department to discuss whether the break room coffee should be medium or dark roast. Democracy is great, but not for everything, Debbie.

How to Politely Decline a Meeting Without Triggering a Workplace Investigation

- **"Can I get the agenda beforehand?"** *Translation: What is this meeting actually about, and why do I need to be there?*

- **"Is this time-sensitive for my current deliverables?"** *Translation: Is this more important than my actual job?*

- **"Would you like me to send my input ahead of time instead?"** *Translation: Let me contribute without sitting through your therapy session.*

- **"I'm at capacity this week, but available next quarter."** *Translation: No, but said professionally enough that you can't complain to HR.*

- **"Happy to be optional on this one!"** *Translation: Please forget I exist for the next hour.*

When You Have to Host a Meeting (The Lesser Evil)

DO:

- Send an agenda that doesn't include "vibes" as a topic
- Set a time limit and actually respect it
- End early if possible (people will literally name their children after you)
- Have a clear purpose that couldn't be achieved via email

DON'T:

- Use it to catch up on every topic since the industrial revolution
- Share your screen if it includes 32 open tabs and your Spotify playlist
- Say "I'll keep this quick" and then don't

- Schedule it during lunch, after 4 PM, or on Friday

Meeting Bingo: Free Space Edition

Create a mental bingo card with these classics:

- "Can you see my screen?"
- "Sorry, I was on mute"
- "We're waiting for one more person" (they're never coming)
- "Let's take this offline"
- "Circle back"
- "Touch base"
- Someone eating loudly
- Technical difficulties that last longer than the actual content
- "Can everyone see the document?" (no one can see the document)

First to get bingo wins... nothing, because you're still stuck in the meeting.

The Meeting Escape Artist's Toolkit

The Ghosting Goodbye Just... stop showing up to recurring meetings and see if anyone notices. If they don't ask after three weeks, you're officially free.

The Strategic Bathroom Break Time it for when the conversation inevitably derails into personal anecdotes about weekend plans.

The Technical Difficulty Excuse "Sorry, I'm having connection issues" works even when your connection is perfect. Use sparingly.

The Hard Stop Power Move "I have a hard stop at [time]" is corporate speak for "I have better things to do" and it's legally bulletproof.

Final Thought

If your meeting doesn't have a goal, a structure, and a clear reason why each person needs to be there, you're not having a meeting—you're hosting a hostage situation with better lighting.

Remember: The most productive meeting is often the one that never happens.

Coming Up Next: Chapter 10 – Team Building Activities and Other Forms of Psychological Warfare

Because nothing builds trust like forced fun, trust falls, and the kind of group activities that make introverts question their career choices.

CHAPTER TEN

Team Building Activities and Other Forms of Psychological Warfare

Because Nothing Says "Trust" Like Mandatory Fun and Matching T-Shirts

Somewhere in the depths of corporate America, someone read an article that said "Teams that play together stay together" and decided to make it everyone else's problem. And just like that, your calendar filled up with trust exercises, icebreakers, and group activities that make you question not just your coworkers, but existence itself.

Welcome to the bizarre world of team building, where introverts suffer, extroverts thrive, and everyone pretends that falling backward into Gary's arms will somehow improve quarterly sales.

Types of Team Building Events (Ranked by How Quickly They Destroy Morale)

1. The Icebreaker Circle of Doom Usually starts with "Let's go around and say our name, role, and a fun fact about ourselves."

Translation: "Let's make everyone uncomfortable before 9 AM."

Fun Facts You'll Hear:

- "I once backpacked through Europe" (they went to London for a long weekend)
- "I collect vintage spoons" (they have three spoons)
- "I have two kids and a dog" (not fun, just facts)

What You Should Say: "My hobby is pretending to enjoy icebreakers while plotting my escape route."

2. The Corporate Scavenger Hunt
A city-wide sprint that turns mild-mannered accountants into competitive maniacs willing to tackle strangers for a photo with a fire hydrant.

Red Flags:

- Someone shows up in athletic gear "just in case"
- Maps are color-coded and laminated
- Prize is a gift card to the office supply store

Survival Strategy: Stick with the middle-of-the-pack people. Avoid overachievers and anyone carrying a whistle.

3. The Trust Fall Tradition
Yes, this still happens. No, it doesn't build trust. What it builds is back pain and a deep understanding of which coworkers have been skipping arm day.

What You're Supposed to Learn: "Team members will support you."

What You Actually Learn: Jerry from Accounting has the upper body strength of a decorative houseplant.

4. The Escape Room Experience
Locked in a room with your coworkers while someone times how long it takes you to want to escape from them instead of the room.

Inevitable Outcomes:

- Someone takes charge immediately (usually the wrong person)
- Arguments about whether the fake key goes in the fake lock
- Watching your manager have a full breakdown over a jigsaw puzzle

5. The Off-Site "Retreat" in a Hotel Conference Room You were promised nature. You got fluorescent lights, stale pastries, and breakout sessions. So many breakout sessions.

Team Exercise: "Design your ideal company culture using craft supplies."

What You're Thinking: "My ideal culture doesn't involve glue sticks or forced creativity."

Corporate Icebreakers No One Wants to Answer

- "What's your biggest fear?" (This isn't therapy, Linda)
- "If you were a kitchen appliance, what would you be?" (A dishwasher because I quietly clean up everyone else's mess)
- "What's something nobody knows about you?" (That I googled "How to fake a family emergency" before this meeting)

How to Survive Team Building Without Losing Your Soul

- **Smile strategically.** People think you're engaged, even if you're mentally drafting your resignation letter in haiku form.
- **Nod at appropriate intervals.** Especially when someone says "synergy" or "collaboration."
- **Volunteer for documentation.** Taking notes looks like participation but mostly involves writing down absurd quotes for later entertainment.
- **Master the phrase "Great insight!"** It's universally applicable and completely meaningless.

Passive-Aggressive Phrases for Team Building Survival

"**I love how energetic everyone is today!**" *Translation: Tone it down, Jennifer. It's 8 AM.*

"**This is such a valuable use of our time!**" *Translation: I could have answered 52 emails in the time it took us to agree on lunch orders.*

"It's so great to get out of the office!" *Translation: Except we're in a rented conference room next to a gas station.*

Team Building Ideas That Should Be Illegal

- Human knot exercises (personal space violations)
- Any activity involving marshmallows (sticky, messy, pointless)
- Trust circles where you share personal information
- Skits (just... no)
- Karaoke disguised as "presentation skills training"
- Mandatory dancing of any kind

If you've participated in more than two of these this quarter, you may be entitled to emotional compensation and a mental health day.

The Team Building Evaluation Form (What You Really Want to Say)

"How did this activity help build trust?" *Real answer: It didn't. If anything, I trust you all less now that I've seen Bob's interpretive dance about quarterly goals.*

"What did you learn about your teammates?" *Real answer: That Sarah takes everything way too seriously and Mike has strong opinions about the proper way to arrange craft supplies.*

"How will you apply these lessons to your daily work?" *Real answer: I will never speak of this again and pretend it never happened.*

Final Thought

Team building shouldn't require trauma counseling afterward. If it does, it wasn't bonding—it was a professionally sanctioned endurance test.

Real team building happens over shared deadlines, successful projects, and the mutual understanding that sometimes work is hard and we're all just trying to make it through the week without crying in the bathroom.

Coming Up Next: Chapter 11 – A Beginner's Guide to Boundary-Setting: Say No Without Saying "F* This Job"

Because "setting healthy limits" is just HR code for "learning how to say no with a smile and a paper trail."

Chapter Eleven

A Beginner's Guide to Boundary-Setting: Say No Without Saying "F* This Job"

The Power of the Polite Decline

Saying "no" at work shouldn't feel like you're launching a nuclear weapon, but somehow it always does. Welcome to the world of professional boundary-setting: the fine art of telling people to back off, buzz off, or do it themselves—without ending up in HR's "needs improvement" column.

This chapter will give you tools to assert your limits gracefully, so you don't burn bridges but maybe scorch the edges just enough to discourage future traffic.

The Signs You're a Recovering People-Pleaser

- You've said "yes" and immediately regretted it... three times today
- Your to-do list looks like a group project for a team you're not actually on
- Someone says "quick favor" and you hear the ominous music from Jaws
- Your coworkers think you're "so reliable" (translation: you're doing their work)
- You've googled "How to say no without hurting feelings" more than once

It's time to break the cycle—with words that sound helpful but mean: Absolutely not.

Phrases That Sound Like Teamwork but Are Actually Boundaries

The Delayed Decline: "Looping back—after reviewing my workload, I won't be able to give this the attention it deserves right now."
Translation: I said nothing for 24 hours so you'd find someone else. It worked.

The Reassignment Redirect: "I'd love to help, but [insert name here] might be better positioned to support this given their recent work on similar projects."
Translation: I have expertly thrown this to someone else. You're welcome.

The Invisible Line in the Sand: "To protect my focus on existing deliverables, I won't be able to take this on. Let's circle back next quarter."
Translation: No. In three months? Also no.

How to Set Boundaries Before You Burn Out

- **Block your calendar.** If you're not unavailable, people will assume you're available. Be mysterious. Be busy. Be booked solid with "strategic planning."

- **Ask questions before agreeing.** "What's the expected time commitment?" is code for: I will vanish if it's over 30 minutes.

- **Don't apologize for having limits.** It's not your fault Gary doesn't understand scope creep or basic project management.

Advanced Boundary Moves

The "I'd Need to Offload Something Else" Play This move forces people to prioritize
Say: "I can take this on, but I'll need to shift something else off my plate—what would you recommend?"
Boom. Now they're in the hot seat, forced to actually think about workload management.

The "Let's Document That" Defense If someone keeps crossing your lines

A BEGINNER'S GUIDE TO BOUNDARY-SETTING: SAY NO... 59

The "Let's Document That" Defense If someone keeps crossing your lines
Say: "Let's summarize expectations in writing so we're aligned moving forward."
Translation: I'm done playing games. The paper trail begins now.

The Boundary Reversal Technique When someone pushes too hard, flip it back
"I'm curious—what's making this feel urgent for you?"
Translation: Please justify your nonsense while I sip this tea and watch you squirm.

Sample Responses for Common Boundary Violations

"Can you stay late to finish this?" *Response:* "I can prioritize this first thing tomorrow morning. What time works for the follow-up?"

"This will only take five minutes." *Response:* "Great! Can you send me the details so I can slot it into my schedule appropriately?"

"You're so good at this, can you just..." *Response:* "Thanks! I'd be happy to walk [other person] through the process so they can handle these going forward."

"I know you're busy, but..." *Response:* "You're right, my bandwidth is pretty tight this week. Let's look at alternatives."

The Boundary-Setting Starter Pack

1. The Calendar Shield: Block time for actual work and label it "Project Focus" or "Deep Work." Treat these blocks as sacred as you would a client meeting.

2. The Response Delay: You don't have to reply immediately to non-urgent requests. Let people sit with their own anxiety for a bit.

3. The Question Deflection: "What's the deadline?" and "Who else is working on this?" are your best friends.

4. The Strategic CC: Loop in relevant people so everyone understands the scope and priorities. Transparency is your shield.

5. The Broken Record Technique: Keep repeating the same boundary in slightly different ways until they get bored and find someone else to bother.

What NOT to Say (Even If You're Thinking It)

- "That's not my job" (technically true, professionally risky)
- "I don't have time for this" (sounds dismissive)
- "Why can't you do it?" (too direct, too honest)
- "This is ridiculous" (save it for your group chat)
- "I'm not your assistant" (accurate, but career-limiting)

Final Thought

Setting boundaries doesn't make you difficult. It makes you professionally evolved. Because at the end of the day, "no" is a complete sentence—it just sounds better with bullet points and a subject line that says "Re: Re: Just Following Up."

Coming Up Next: Chapter 12 – How to Quit Mentally Without Getting Fired Physically

Because sometimes the only thing keeping you going is the thought of not going at all.

CHAPTER TWELVE

How to Quit Mentally Without Getting Fired Physically

Keep Collecting That Paycheck While Your Soul Escapes Through Your Eyes

Sometimes you don't actually quit your job. You just slowly stop caring until you're technically employed but spiritually freelancing. And that, dear reader, is what we call Corporate Ghost Mode.

In this chapter, you'll learn how to gracefully disengage while still appearing "committed," "present," and "open to feedback"—even though you've mentally clocked out and are currently planning your escape to a cabin in the woods where the Wi-Fi doesn't reach (or interviewing for a new job).

A WORD FROM OUR SPONSORS: If you are at this "quiet quitting" stage, it's a clear sign you should be become best friends with the LinkedIn Jobs board. The ideas given here are partly for humor, partly for making life bearable until you can pack up and leave. If the first 11 chapters of this book haven't helped, it's might be time to find a new set of coworkers.

Signs You've Already Quit (Mentally)

- You refer to every task as "corporate BS"
- You've attended three meetings today and retained exactly zero information
- Your work wardrobe has devolved into "whatever's clean-ish"
- You respond to everything with "Sounds good" regardless of whether it sounds good

- You get irrationally angry when someone schedules a meeting with an actual purpose
- You've started rating your days based on how little you had to pretend to care

The Art of "Performative Engagement"

When you've given up, but HR must never know.

Eye Contact and Strategic Nodding If you're on Zoom, look near your webcam every 30-45 seconds. Bonus points for furrowing your brow when someone says "deliverables" or "synergies."

Say Things That Sound Productive Even when you're mentally googling "can you live off the grid with no money," throw out corporate classics:

- "I think we're close to a breakthrough here"
- "Let's circle back after I digest this"
- "Would love to get some cross-functional input"

These phrases mean nothing. That's why they're perfect.

Email Templates for the Mentally Checked Out

1. The "I'm Responding but Not Committing" Special:

Thanks for the update—looping in [someone else] for visibility. Let's revisit early next week. Hope that works!

Translation: I've yeeted this into someone else's inbox and I'm never thinking about it again.

2. The "I'm Here, But Emotionally Not" Classic:

Appreciate the heads-up. Let me sit with this and get back to you soon.

Translation: I will never think about this again.

3. The "Yes, and Please Go Away" Masterpiece:

HOW TO QUIT MENTALLY WITHOUT GETTING FIRED...

Great idea—feel free to take the lead and keep us posted!

Translation: This is your problem now. Forever.

Tasks You Can Do While Doing Absolutely Nothing

- Replying to emails with "Sounds good!"
- Creating folders with vague titles like "Q4 Strategy Stuff"
- Highlighting text in shared documents to show "engagement"
- Reformatting presentations for the fifth time
- Volunteering to "own the notes" (ultimate low-effort, high-visibility move)
- Rewriting Teams messages six times and sending none of them

Advanced Mental Quitter Moves

1. "Working on Strategy" This means you're thinking. About what? Nobody knows. But it's impossible to measure and sounds vital to business operations.

2. "Heads-Down Day" Block your calendar with fake focus time so nobody can schedule meetings. Watch documentaries about people who escaped corporate life and now make cheese in Vermont.

3. "Light Bandwidth This Week" Say it early, say it often. Then proceed to do the same amount of work, but with more sighs and strategic bathroom breaks.

Warning: Don't Over-Commit to Under-Commitment

If you stop responding altogether, people will notice. The golden rule: Stay engaged enough to be forgotten, but not enough to be promoted.

You want to hit that sweet spot where they say: "Wait, are they still here?" And someone else responds: "I think so. They cc'd me on something last week."

Mission accomplished.

The Gradual Boundary Expansion Technique

Week 1: "I'll need to check my calendar"
Week 3: "Let me see if I have bandwidth"
Week 6: "I'm pretty booked this month"
Week 10: "My Q4 is completely locked up"
Week 15: You've achieved legendary status as someone who's always "slammed" but no one can quite remember with what

How to Look Busy While Doing Nothing

- Have multiple browser tabs open (include one spreadsheet for credibility)

- Walk around the office carrying papers and looking slightly concerned

- Use phrases like "I'm waiting to hear back from..." (you're not waiting for anything)

- Schedule mysterious one-hour blocks titled "Client Calls" (it's your lunch break)

- Master the art of looking thoughtfully frustrated at your computer screen

Mental Quitter's Daily Affirmations

- "This too shall pass... hopefully by 5 PM"

- "I am not my job, my job is not me"

- "Every paycheck is one step closer to freedom"

- "I can survive anything for eight hours a day"

- "My coworkers' urgency is not my emergency"

Final Thought

Sometimes the best form of conflict resolution is emotional detachment. Be present in body, be polite in demeanor, but let your spirit roam free—preferably somewhere with better coffee and fewer acronyms.

You're not giving up; you're conserving energy for things that actually matter. Like planning your actual escape route.

You made it to the end of "Help! My Coworkers Are Driving Me Crazy"—a journey through corporate chaos, polite warfare, and how to survive coworkers who deserve to be left on read forever.

You're now equipped with the tools to identify workplace toxicity, respond with professional grace, and maintain your sanity in an environment designed to test it daily. Use these powers wisely, document everything, and remember: it's definitely not you.

Now go forth and prosper, armed with the knowledge that you can handle anything your coworkers throw at you—as long as you have good Wi-Fi, strong coffee, and an exit strategy.

May your meetings be brief, your emails be clear, and your coworkers be tolerable.

If you enjoy this book, please consider leaving a review on amazon.com. Thank you!

www.ingramcontent.com/pod-product-compliance
Lightning Source LLC
Chambersburg PA
CBHW052123070526
44586CB00016B/2061